YEAR 1

sworks

Fiction and Poetry Texts

Julie Orrell

Published in 2004 by:
Nelson Thornes Ltd
Delta Place
27 Bath Road
CHELTENHAM
GL53 7TH
United Kingdom

04 05 06 07 08 / 10 9 8 7 6 5 4 3 2 1

A catalogue record for this book is available from the British Library

ISBN 0-7487-8645-7

Illustrations by Cathy Hughes, Mike Phillips and Woody Fox
Page make-up by GreenGate Publishing Services

Printed in Great Britain by Ashford Colour Press

Acknowledgements

All texts written by and copyright Julie Orrell except:

'Sand' Copyright © 1991 John Foster, first published in *Four O'Clock Friday* (Oxford University Press); *Lion at School and Other Stories* by Philippa Pearce (Viking 1985) Copyright © Philippa Pearce 1985; extract from 'Sally and the Magic Rattle' from *The Listening Corner Storybook* Copyright © Joyce Dunbar 1986 Reproduced by permission of David Higham Associates; 'Boa Constrictor' from *Where the Sidewalk Ends* by Shel Silverstein Copyright © 1974 by Evil Eye Music, Inc.; renewed 2002 by Evil Eye, LLC, by permission of Edite Kroll Literary Agency Inc; 'The Three Little Pigs' by Marian Swinger, taken from *The Works*, by permission of Macmillan Children's Books (2000); 'Goldilocks' letter to the three bears' and 'Goldilocks' envelope' from *The Jolly Postman* Copyright © Allan and Janet Ahlberg 1986 (Viking 1999); Text and illustration from 'Here Come the Aliens!' by Colin McNaughton Copyright © 1995 Colin McNaughton reproduced by permission of Walker Books Ltd, London, SE11 5HJ; 'The Bed Book' Copyright © Sylvia Plath reproduced by permission of Faber and Faber Ltd; 'The Cat's Tongue' from *Blackberry Ink* by Eve Merriam Copyright © 1985 Eve Merriam and used by permission of Marian Reiner; 'Miss Tibbles' Copyright © Ian Serraillier Reproduced by permission of Anne Serraillier; 'Cats Sleep Anywhere' by Eleanor Farjeon taken from the book *Blackbird has Spoken* published by Macmillan Children's Books and reproduced by permission of David Higham Associates, London.

Cover image: C506.550078 Corel 506 (NT)

Every effort has been made to trace the copyright holders but if any have been inadvertently overlooked, the publishers will be pleased to make the necessary arrangement at the first opportunity.

Contents

How to use this book

What this book contains

- Extracts from published works, plus tailor-made extracts, all arranged and chosen specifically to match the examples of medium-term planning provided by the National Literacy Strategy
- Teaching ideas for each extract to get you started, covering some of the relevant text, sentence or word level objectives from the relevant unit

How you can use *Classworks Literacy Texts* with other resources

- The blocked unit structure means you can dip into the book to find resources perfect for what you're teaching this week – it doesn't matter what plan, scheme or other resource you're using
- There are two *Classworks Literacy Texts* books for every year from Reception (or Primary 1) to Year 6 (or Primary 7): one contains Fiction and Poetry, the other contains Non-fiction. Both books together contain texts for every unit of the medium-term plans

What each page does

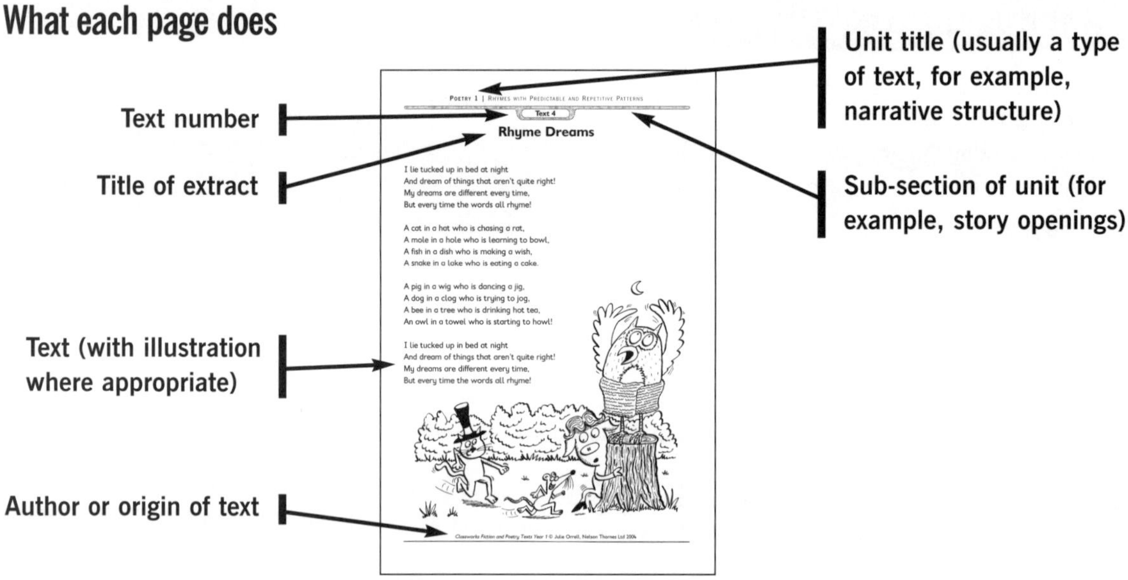

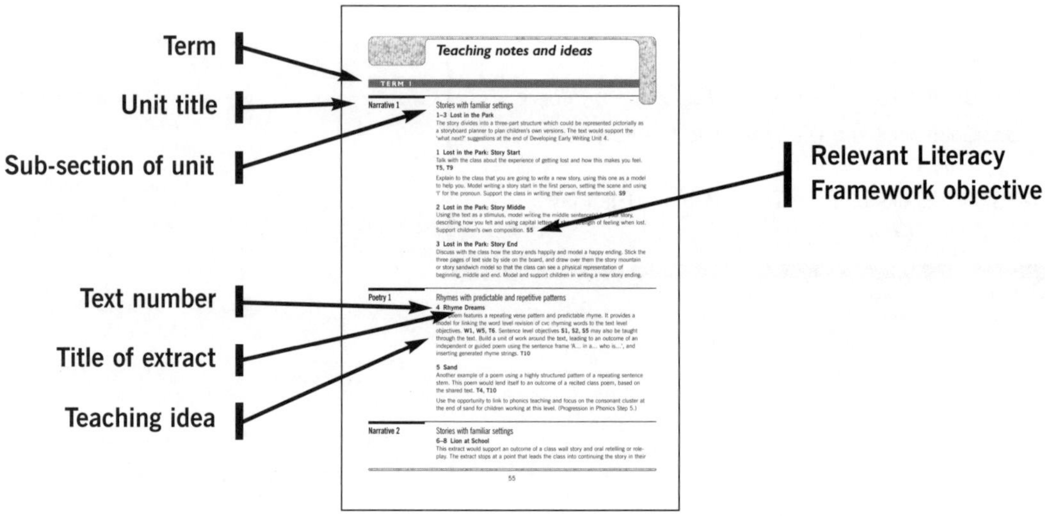

Text 1

Lost in the Park

Story Start

It was a bright, sunny day and Phoebe's mum had been promising to take her to the park for ages. "Mum…" sang Phoebe, "Can we go to the park today? Please, please, please?"

They left behind all the Saturday jobs and escaped to the park. It was a brilliant park near Phoebe's house. It had all the best apparatus to play on: swings, a slide, a huge climbing frame in the shape of a rocket and a commando slide. The commando slide was Phoebe's favourite, it had a big, black, bouncy tyre which you sat on and swung down the wire like Tarzan.

Phoebe ran off to play, while Mum sat on the old wooden bench with cracked green paint to watch.

Two of Phoebe's friends were at the park that day, Billy and Andrew. They had a competition to see who could swing highest on the swings. The old, cold metal chains of the swings creaked as they swung higher and higher until they could almost touch the clouds. It felt like peeping into the land at the top of the beanstalk and Phoebe half expected to hear the "Fee, fi, fo, fum" of a giant calling.

Next they ran to the commando slide and swooped over wild jungle clearings on twisted vines. Parrots squawked overhead and monkeys sat hunched in the branches, watching them with round eyes.

Text 2

Lost in the Park

Story Middle

After a while, the children decided to play hide and seek. A winding path led from the park out into a wild area of trees and bushes which stretched as far as the eye could see. Phoebe ran off to hide first, down the winding path and into the trees. Further and further she ran, always looking for exactly the right spot to hide. Soon she was far away from the playground and in a part of the wood she had never seen before.

Phoebe found the perfect hiding place, curled up in the cave made by the root of a giant tree. Nobody would find her there, she thought.

From time to time Phoebe heard the faraway voices of her friends as they tried to find her, but nobody came this far into the woods.

She began to feel a little bit worried – if nobody found her, would she be able to find her way back? Carefully, she squeezed herself out from the secret cave and looked around. Paths led off in several directions and Phoebe realised that she had no idea which path would take her back to her mum in the park. She ran helter-skelter down first one path… then another, but none of them looked right.

She was lost! Phoebe felt salty tears beginning to well up in her eyes. “MUM!” she shouted, “HELP!”

Text 3

Lost in the Park

Story End

"Are you all right, dear?" asked a voice behind her. Phoebe looked around and saw that it was Mrs Peters, the dinner lady from school.

"Oh, Mrs Peters," sobbed Phoebe, "I'm lost and I can't find my way back to the park."

"Come with me, I'm heading that way and we'll make sure we get you back to your mum".

A few minutes later, Phoebe started to recognise the view from the path and before long they were back. Phoebe gave her mum a big hug and Mrs Peters a big smile.

Text 4

Rhyme Dreams

I lie tucked up in bed at night
And dream of things that aren't quite right!
My dreams are different every time,
But every time the words all rhyme!

A cat in a hat who is chasing a rat,
A mole in a hole who is learning to bowl,
A fish in a dish who is making a wish,
A snake in a lake who is eating a cake.

A pig in a wig who is dancing a jig,
A dog in a clog who is trying to jog,
A bee in a tree who is drinking hot tea,
An owl in a towel who is starting to howl!

I lie tucked up in bed at night
And dream of things that aren't quite right!
My dreams are different every time,
But every time the words all rhyme!

Text 5

Sand

Sand in your fingernails
Sand between your toes
Sand in your earholes
Sand up your nose!

Sand in your sandwiches
Sand on your bananas
Sand in your bed at night
Sand in your pyjamas!

Sand in your sandals
Sand in your hair
Sand in your knickers
Sand everywhere!

John Foster

Text 6

Lion at School

Story Start

Once upon a time there was a little girl who didn't like going to school. She always set off late. Then she had to hurry, but she never hurried fast enough.

One morning she was hurrying along as usual when she turned a corner and there stood a lion, blocking her way. He stood waiting for her. He stared at her with his yellow eyes. He growled, and when he growled the little girl could see that his teeth were as sharp as skewers and knives. He growled: "I'm going to eat you up."

"Oh dear!" said the little girl, and she began to cry.

"Wait!" said the lion. "I haven't finished. I'm going to eat you up UNLESS you take me to school with you."

"Oh, dear!" said the little girl. "I couldn't do that. My teacher says we mustn't bring pets to school."

"I'm not a pet," said the lion. He growled again, and she saw that his tail swished from side to side in anger – *swish! swash! swish! swash!* "You can tell your teacher that I'm a friend who is coming to school with you," he said. "Now shall we go?"

Philippa Pearce

Text 7

Lion at School

Story Middle

The little girl had stopped crying. She said: “All right. But you must promise two things. First of all, you mustn’t eat anyone: it’s not allowed.”

“I suppose I can growl?” said the lion.

“I suppose you can,” said the little girl.

“And I suppose I can roar?”

“Must you?” said the little girl.

“Yes,” said the lion.

“Then I suppose you can,” said the little girl.

“And what’s the second thing?” asked the lion.

“You must let me ride on your back to school.”

“Very well,” said the lion.

He crouched down on the pavement and the little girl climbed on his back. She held on by his mane. Then they went on together towards the school, the little girl riding the lion.

The lion ran with the little girl on his back to school. Even so, they were late. The little girl and the lion went into the classroom just as the teacher was calling the register.

Philippa Pearce

Text 8

Lion at School

Story End

The teacher stopped calling the register when she saw the little girl and the lion. She stared at the lion, and all the other children stared at the lion, wondering what the teacher was going to say. The teacher said to the little girl: "You know you are not allowed to bring pets into school."

The lion began to swish his tail – *swish! swash!* The little girl said quickly: "This is not a pet. This is my friend who is coming to school with me."

The teacher stared at the lion, but she said to the little girl: "What is his name then?"

"Noil," said the little girl. "His name is Noil. Just Noil." She knew it would be no good to tell the teacher that her friend was a lion, so she had turned his name backwards: LION – NOIL.

The teacher wrote the name down in the register: NOIL. Then she finished calling the register.

"Betty Small," she said.

"Yes," said the little girl.

"Noil," said the teacher.

"Yes," said the lion. He mumbled, opening his mouth as little as possible, so the teacher should not see his teeth as sharp as skewers and knives. He did not swish his tail. He did not growl. He sat next to the little girl as good as gold.

All that morning the lion sat up on his chair next to the little girl, like a big cat, with his tail curled round his front paws, as good as gold. No one saw his teeth, no one saw his claws. He didn't speak unless the teacher spoke to him. He didn't growl, he didn't roar.

Philippa Pearce

Text 9

Sally and the magic rattle: the shore-people

Story Start

Do you have a favourite place to hide? Sally does. In her parents' bedroom, between two wardrobes, is a big mirror with a shelf, and underneath the shelf hangs a curtain pulled across to make a little cupboard for shoes and slippers. That's where Sally goes to be on her own, to think and dream.

Sally has a secret too. She has a magic rattle. It was given to her as a farewell present by an old lady who used to live in the same block of flats. Sally had been watching the removal van from her balcony three floors up, waiting to wave goodbye, when the old lady had called to her.

She had presented Sally with an old silver rattle. "For me?" asked Sally, thinking it must be meant for Tim, her baby brother.

"For you," answered the old lady. "It's a magic rattle. You must close your eyes, shake the rattle and say these words:

'Rattle me, rattle me,
Roll me around.
Close your eyes,
Hear my sound.
Let me take you
Where I will,
Under the ground,
Over the hill.'"

Sally thanked the old lady very much and ran off with the rattle – to her cupboard of course, where she wouldn't be disturbed. Making a little space for herself amongst the shoes, she closed her eyes, repeated the words and gently shook the rattle.

Joyce Dunbar

Text 10

Sally and the magic rattle: the shore-people

Story Middle

What did she hear? It was the sound of the sea! She opened her eyes and blinked in surprise.

For Sally was no longer in the dark bedroom cupboard but dazzled by sunlight on a lovely sandy shore. In her hand was the magic rattle; beside her a bucket and spade.

She got to work straight away building a sandcastle. She built turrets and a courtyard and a moat with a bridge. Then she paddled barefoot by the water's edge collecting seaweed and shells to decorate the castle. It was the best she'd ever made. She had just put in a seashell for the door when it opened wide!

"Come in, come in," said a little voice. "Tea is on the table."

A crab stood holding the door. "Come on in," he said again. "The shore-people are waiting."

"Who are they?" asked Sally.

"The people who live on the sea-shore, of course," replied the crab.

Sally walked through the door of the castle she had built, which had grown mysteriously bigger (or perhaps she had grown much smaller) and found herself in a banqueting hall with shell-shaped windows and seaweed drapes. There sat shore-lords and shore-ladies, round a table of mother-of-pearl. A place was laid specially for Sally.

"Have some seaweed soup," said a shore-lord.

"And some jelly-fish jelly," said a shore-lady.

"And a sand sandwich," said a shrimp who waited on them.

Sally was about to taste the jelly-fish jelly when everyone jumped up from the table. "Run!" shouted a shore-lord. "The tide's coming in!"

Joyce Dunbar

Text 11

Sally and the magic rattle: the shore-people

Story End

Sure enough, through the door and all the windows, the sea was flooding the castle. Sally ran with the shore-people across the bridge, over the moat, away from the incoming tide.

The shore-people looked sad. Some were weeping quietly. "This is always happening," they said. "No sooner do we settle down in a nice new castle than the tide drives us out. If only you children would build them further inland."

"That was the best we ever had."

"Never mind," said Sally. "I'll build you a better one, here, away from the tide."

And so she did. The shore-people were so pleased. "You must be our guest of honour," they said to Sally, and dressed her in a turquoise gown. Shells were sounded like trumpets and Sally shook her rattle as she led the way through the door of the new castle… straight into her parents' bedroom.

"Where have you been, Sally?" said her mother. "I've been looking everywhere for you. And what are you doing in my turquoise dress? Take it off and go and play with Tim while I get tea ready."

In the furthest corner of the cupboard, Sally hid the magic rattle. "Look, Tim," she said to her brother, "I've brought you a seashell…"

Joyce Dunbar

Text 12

Boa Constrictor

Oh, I'm being eaten
By a boa constrictor,
A boa constrictor,
A boa constrictor,
I'm being eaten by a boa constrictor,
And I don't like it – one bit.
Well, what do you know?
It's nibblin' my toe.
Oh, gee,
It's up to my knee.
Oh my,
It's up to my thigh.
Oh, fiddle,
It's up to my middle.
Oh, heck,
It's up to my neck.
Oh, dread,
It upmmmmmmmmmffffffff…

Shel Silverstein

Text 13

Jack and the Beanstalk

Part One

Once upon a time there lived a young lad called Jack. He lived with his mother in an old stone cottage with little money to make ends meet.

"Jack, my lad," said his mother one day, "the time has come for us to sell the old white cow. We have nothing in the pantry to eat and Daisy will fetch us gold enough to last till Christmastide." So the very next day Jack set off on the path to market, leading Daisy the cow on a piece of rope.

Well, he hadn't gone very far when he met a little old man carrying a red spotted handkerchief on a stick over his shoulder.

"That's a fine looking cow you have there," he said to Jack. "'Tis a shame to send her to market. Give me the cow and I'll give you something that money can't buy." Unfurling his spotted handkerchief, the old man shook five cream-coloured beans into the palm of Jack's hand. "Magic beans, these are," whispered the man, "just you wait and see."

Jack raced home to show his mother the magic beans.

"You great dollop!" shouted his mother, for she knew that they would not feed hungry bellies. And with that she threw the beans out of the window into the cabbage patch.

Text 14

Jack and the Beanstalk

Part Two

When Jack awoke the next morning, his room was as black as night. Jack peered out of his bedroom window and looked up. A tangle of stems and branches strangled the cottage so thickly that sunlight could not creep through. A giant beanstalk stretched up, up, up – high into the sky so that the very tip of the beanstalk disappeared into the clouds.

Without thinking twice, Jack started to climb the beanstalk. At the very top of the beanstalk he discovered a land above the clouds. He stepped carefully off the beanstalk ladder, touching the clouds first with the tip of his toe to make sure that they would bear his weight. Ahead of him was a wooden signpost, bearing the words: 'To the castle'.

Jack followed the sign and soon he found himself at the gates of a huge stone castle. He crept in through a tiny gap in the enormous door. Sitting at the giant table in the giant kitchen was the biggest woman Jack had ever seen.

"What do you want here?" asked the big woman. "My husband is a giant, and he will eat you up as soon as look at you…"

Suddenly, Jack heard giant footsteps and a huge voice echoing like the rumble of thunder. Quick as a flash, Jack jumped into the oven and hid. A great hairy giant stomped into the kitchen and sniffed the air, hungrily.

"Fee, fi, fo, fum,
I smell the blood of an Englishman.
Be he alive or be he dead,
I'll grind his bones to make my bread!"

Jack sat trembling in the oven as he heard the giant's wife say, "Sit yourself down and stop fretting. 'Tis nothing but your breakfast warming."

When the giant had finished his breakfast, his wife brought him a heavy sack, full to the brim with gold. Jack's eyes grew as big as saucers, for he had never seen such a mountain of gold before. Then, when he had counted his coins, the giant lay back in his chair and went to sleep.

Jack saw his chance and jumped out of the oven, grabbed the gold and ran as fast as his young legs would carry him. Helter skelter down the beanstalk he flew, down… down… down and home to his cottage. Jack and his mother lived happily for many months, but Jack could never forget the Giant's castle, and the day came when he decided to climb the beanstalk once more.

Text 15

Jack and the Beanstalk

Part Three

This time when he reached the castle, the giant's wife was again busy in the kitchen. Jack climbed the vine beside the door and swung on the great brass door knocker. He heard the sound echoing inside the castle. When the giant's wife came to the door, she stared down at Jack and asked, "Hmmm, haven't I seen you before? Weren't you the lad who ran off with our gold?"

"Oh no," replied Jack, and with that he darted into the kitchen. Before long, he heard again the thunder of the giant returning for his dinner. Quick as a flash, Jack jumped into the meat safe and hid.

"Fee, fi, fo, fum,
I smell the blood of an Englishman!
Be he alive or be he dead,
I'll grind his bones to make my bread!" roared the giant.

"'Tis only your dinner cooking," muttered his wife, setting a giant plate of stew before him.

When he had finished eating, the giant said, "Bring me my hen!"

Jack could hardly believe his eyes when he saw the big red hen that was placed on the table before the giant.

"Lay," said the giant. The hen clucked loudly then laid an egg on the table. But not an ordinary egg, for this egg was smooth and shiny and of the purest gold.

As soon as the giant settled his head on his hands to rest, Jack raced from the meat safe and grabbed the hen that laid the golden eggs and ran as fast as his young legs would carry him. Helter skelter down the beanstalk he flew, down… down… down and home to his cottage.

Do you think Jack was content with his golden hen? Well, for a while he and his mother lived happily on the eggs of gold that the hen provided. But the day came when Jack decided he would go up the beanstalk just one more time, to see what other treasures were to be found at the giant's castle.

Text 16

Jack and the Beanstalk

Part Four

As he had before, Jack hid himself away in the kitchen when he heard the sound of thunder bringing the giant home for his tea.

"Fee, fi, fo, fum,
I smell the blood of an Englishman!
Be he alive or be he dead,
I'll grind his bones to make my bread!" roared the giant, peering under the table.

"Well, if it is the same lad as before, he'll be hiding in the oven," replied the wife. Luckily Jack was not hiding in the oven this time, but in the pantry. The giant ate his giant tea and asked for his golden harp.

Now, a harp is an instrument that makes beautiful music and a *golden* harp makes the most beautiful music you have ever heard. More beautiful than the song of birds in the early morning, more beautiful than the sound of clear water tinkling over the rocks in a mountain stream. Very soon, the golden harp had lulled the giant into a deep sleep with its magical notes.

Quick as a flash, Jack slipped out of the pantry and grabbed the harp under his arm. He ran towards the door but…

"MASTER! MASTER!" shouted the harp, and the giant woke with a start.

Jack ran as fast as his little legs would carry him… out of the castle… through the clouds… to the very tip of the beanstalk. He swung down the beanstalk, down, down towards his mother's garden. But the beanstalk began to shake as if it were being tossed in a terrible storm. Looking up, Jack saw giant boots above his head. Quick as a flash, he swung down into the garden and, grabbing an axe from the woodshed, CHOPPED at the beanstalk for all he was worth. With a noise like the crash of thunder, the giant fell down dead as a doornail as the beanstalk came falling from the sky and toppled into Jack's garden.

Jack and his mother lived the rest of their lives happily ever after, with the red hen to lay golden eggs and the golden harp to play beautiful music. Jack never saw the stranger again, though he never forgot the land above the clouds and his adventures at the top of the beanstalk.

Character Profile – Writing Frame

Character profile

Name:
Address:
Age:
Description:
Likes:
Dislikes:

Important information:

Text 18

Character Profile – Big Bad Wolf

WANTED

Have you seen this wolf?

Name: Big Bad Wolf
Address: Woodcutters' Forest
Description: Lean, mean, hairy and hungry
Likes: Eating cakes, girls and grannies
Dislikes: Being locked in cupboards, woodcutters with axes

Wanted in connection with: impersonating a granny

REWARD OFFERED!

If you see this wolf in a forest near you, contact your local police station or call Wolfstoppers on 02102598.

Text 19

Character Profile – Troll

WANTED

Have you seen this troll?

Name: Terrible Troll
Address: Under the rickety wooden bridge
Description: Long, shaggy hair and beard, sharp claws and teeth, hungry, loud roar
Likes: Goat stew
Dislikes: Noisy goats trip-trapping over his bridge

Wanted in connection with: threatening behaviour and bullying billy-goats.

REWARD OFFERED!

If you see this troll in a river near you, contact your local police station or call Trollstoppers on 02102598.

Text 20

The Three Little Pigs

The first little pig in a house of straw
heard a tap tap tap on her little green door.
"Little pig, little pig, let me come in,"
said the big bad wolf with a big bad grin.
Then he huffed and he puffed and he huffed some more
and down went the little pig's house of straw.
The next little pig was taking a nap
in her house of sticks when she heard a tap
and the big bad wolf with a big bad grin
gave a huff and a puff and blew her house in.
Then the big bad wolf, still up to his tricks
went off to the third little house of bricks.
"Little pig, little pig, let me come in,"
said the big bad wolf with a big bad grin.
And he huffed and he puffed till his face turned red.
"My house is too tough," the little pig said.
"I'll come down the chimney," the wolf yelled, "Now!"
But the fire was lit and the wolf yelled "Ow!"
and shot straight out in a cloud of smoke
as the third little pig gave the fire a poke.
Then the wolf blew on his paws with a huff and a puff
and he hobbled off home. He'd had enough.

Marian Swinger

Text 21

Twinkle, Twinkle, Little Star
and
Twinkle, Twinkle, Little Bat

Twinkle, twinkle, little star,
How I wonder what you are!
Up above the world so high,
Like a diamond in the sky!
Twinkle, twinkle, little star,
How I wonder what you are!

Anon

Twinkle, twinkle, little bat!
How I wonder what you're at!
Up above the world you fly,
Like a tea-tray in the sky.
Twinkle, twinkle little bat!
How I wonder what you're at.

Lewis Carroll

Writing frame

Twinkle, twinkle, little ______________________ ,
How I wonder what ____________ ____________ !
Up above the world ____________ ____________ ,
Like a ____________ in the sky.
Twinkle, twinkle little ______________________ ,
How I wonder what ____________ ____________ .

Text 22

What are Little Girls Made of?

What are little girls made of?
What are little girls made of?
Sugar and spice
And all things nice
That's what little girls are made of.

What are little boys made of?
What are little boys made of?
Frogs and snails
And puppy-dogs' tails
That's what little boys are made of.

Anon

Text 23

Medio Pollito

Story Start

Once upon a time, a beautiful black hen was sitting on her eggs in the heat of the Spanish sun. One by one, the eggs cracked and out popped a huge brood of chicks. Now the very last egg to hatch had an unusual chick inside – for this chick looked just as if he had been cut in half. He was just as beautiful as all his brothers and sisters, but he looked very different. This little chick had just one eye, one wing, one leg and one half a body. Because of this, Mother Hen called him Medio Pollito, which means "half a chick" in Spanish.

Medio Pollito was a clever little chick and he was soon the boss of the brood. But Medio Pollito was also a naughty little chick. When it was time to walk to the river to drink, Medio Pollito would hide in the olive trees and pretend that he couldn't hear Mother Hen calling. When it was time to go back to the roost for the night, Medio Pollito would always be the last.

One sunny day he hopped over to Mother Hen and chirped, "I'm bored in this dusty farmyard. I want something more exciting, I'm going to Madrid to see the King of Spain."

Although Mother Hen warned him that his journey would be full of dangers, Medio Pollito took no notice and set off to find the King of Spain. Mother Hen watched him go with a tear in her beady eye and as he hopped away she called, "Remember, Medio Pollito, you must be kind and polite to everyone you meet."

But Medio Pollito pretended that he couldn't hear her and went on his way.

Text 24

Medio Pollito

Story Middle

Before long, he came to a stream where the water was thick with weed. "Medio Pollito," called the stream, "please help me! I need these weeds cleared away so that my water can run freely again."

"Oh no," sneered Medio Pollito, "for I am off to see the King of Spain. I will not help you." And Medio Pollito shook his shiny feathers in the Spanish sun and hopped on.

A little while later, he came across a smouldering fire. "Medio Pollito," whispered the fire, "please help me. Put some sticks on me so that I do not die."

"Oh no," sneered Medio Pollito, "for I am off to see the King of Spain. I will not help you." And Medio Pollito shook his shiny feathers in the Spanish sun and hopped on.

The next day Medio Pollito could see the fine city of Madrid in the distance. On the road to Madrid, he passed a big chestnut tree with the wind in its branches.

"Medio Pollito," howled the wind, "please help me. I am trapped in the branches of the chestnut tree and I cannot escape!"

"Oh no," sneered Medio Pollito, "for I am off to see the King of Spain. I will not help you." And Medio Pollito shook his shiny feathers in the Spanish sun and hopped on.

The chicken had no difficulty in spotting the King's palace, for it was the most beautiful building he had ever seen. Towers of golden stone glowed in the sunshine and steps of marble led up to the doorway.

Medio Pollito settled down to wait by the steps but the king's head chef spotted him and grabbed him, thinking he would make a tasty soup. He threw Medio Pollito into a huge pot full of water.

Text 25

Medio Pollito

Story End

"Water, water, help me, please," cried the chicken, who didn't like getting wet.

"Why should I help you now, when you didn't help when I needed you to clear the weeds?" asked the water.

"Fire, fire, help me, please," cried the chicken, for the water was getting hot.

"Why should I help you now, when you left me to die out in the forest?" asked the fire.

Just then, the head chef took off the lid to check on his soup. A great gust of wind swept Medio Pollito out of the pot, out of the window and up into the air.

"Wind, wind, help me, please," cried the chicken, who was now being tossed high above the rooftops.

"Why should I help you now, when you left me trapped in the chestnut tree?" asked the wind, and he swept the chicken high up to the top of the tallest church in the city of Madrid. Carefully, very carefully, the wind fastened Medio Pollito onto the top of the steeple which, after all, was no less than he deserved.

And there he remains to this day. He stands swinging in the wind, balancing on his one leg and looking out over Madrid with his one eye and wishing that he had listened to Mother Hen's advice.

Text 26

Goldilocks and the Three Bears

Story Start

Once upon a time there lived three bears. Their names were Daddy Bear (he was the biggest), Mummy Bear (she was middle sized) and Baby Bear (he was the smallest). They lived in a tumbledown cottage, deep in the woods. At the edge of the woods there lived a little girl who had long, flowing golden hair. Her parents called her Goldilocks.

One spring morning, Goldilocks was playing in her garden when she heard a bird singing in the woods. The song was so beautiful that Goldilocks decided to follow the song and find the singing bird. Now, Goldilocks's mummy had told her many times that it was very dangerous to wander off on her own, but Goldilocks was not very good at listening to advice. She unlatched the green wooden gate and tiptoed off down the grassy track into the woods.

At about the same time, the Bear family decided to go for an early morning stroll in the woods while their breakfast porridge cooled down, for it was far too hot to eat. They strolled through the woods, Mummy and Daddy Bear marched ahead while Baby Bear skipped along behind.

Text 27

Goldilocks and the Three Bears

Story Middle (1)

Goldilocks ventured deeper and deeper into the woods, far further than she had ever been before with her mummy. Try as she might, she couldn't see the singing bird. The further she went, the further ahead the song seemed to be, always just out of reach, like the end of a rainbow. She had left the grassy track long ago and was very lost.

Just as she was beginning to give up hope of finding the path again, Goldilocks stumbled upon the cottage belonging to the three bears. The door was open, so Goldilocks peeped inside. There was no sign of anyone in the kitchen so Goldilocks crept in to have a good look around. A delicious smell wafted from three bowls arranged on a table covered with a red and white chequered tablecloth.

"Mmmm... porridge," whispered Goldilocks. It was her favourite breakfast, and she was very hungry.

Text 28

Goldilocks and the Three Bears

Story Middle (2)

Then Goldilocks did another thing that her mummy would not have liked. She took a taste from the first bowl, which was big and full.

"Too hot," she exclaimed. Next, Goldilocks tasted the second bowl, with roses around the rim.

"Too cold!" she muttered. The third bowl was made of white china, with a pattern of pawprints around the rim.

"Mmmmmmm, just right," she smiled, and polished the bowl clean.

"I think I'll just have a little rest – I'm sure no one will mind," said Goldilocks to herself. Arranged around the table were three chairs. The first chair was huge. It was carved out of oak and was so high that Goldilocks had to clamber up onto it. "Too hard," she thought, and tried the next chair.

The second chair was low and soft, covered in red velvet with buttons of brass. Goldilocks sank in, but quickly climbed out again. "Too soft," she thought, and tried the next chair.

The third chair was small and straight, carved of wood and with a rush seat. As soon as Goldilocks sat down, she knew that this was just the chair for her. But with a horrible splintering sound, – CRACK! – the wood split and the little wooden chair collapsed and Goldilocks fell with a BUMP on the floor.

By now, Goldilocks was so tired that she crept up the creaking staircase, looking for a comfortable bed to take a nap. In the bedroom she found three beds. The first bed was tall and high, with posts at the corners. Goldilocks climbed up, but, "Too hard," she thought.

The second bed had a saggy mattress and an eiderdown of patchwork. Goldilocks sank into the bed, but she could not get comfortable. "Too soft," she thought.

The third bed was just Goldilocks's height and had a blue blanket with a little bear embroidered in one corner. Goldilocks snuggled down on the bed and before very long she was fast asleep.

Text 29

Goldilocks and the Three Bears

Story End

Meanwhile, the bears had finished their walk and arrived back at the cottage. As soon as they entered, they could see that something was wrong.

"**Somebody's been eating MY porridge!**" roared Daddy Bear, in a big voice.

"Somebody's been eating MY porridge," exclaimed Mummy Bear, in a middle-sized voice.

"**Somebody's been eating my porridge – and they've eaten it all up!**" wailed Baby Bear, in a little voice.

The bears looked at the chairs.

"**Somebody's been sitting in MY chair!**" roared Daddy Bear in a big voice.

"Somebody's been sitting in MY chair," exclaimed Mummy Bear in a middle-sized voice.

"**Somebody's been sitting in my chair and they've b-b-b-broken it!**" wailed Baby Bear, in a little voice.

The three bears marched upstairs.

"**Somebody's been sleeping in MY bed!**" roared Daddy Bear, in a big voice.

"Somebody's been sleeping in MY bed," exclaimed Mummy Bear, in a middle-sized voice.

"**Somebody's been sleeping in my bed – and she's still there!**" wailed Baby Bear, in a little voice.

At the sound of the bears' voices so close to her, Goldilocks woke with a start. She opened her eyes to see three furry faces staring down at her. Quick as a flash, she jumped out of bed, ran down the stairs and out into the sunshine. She didn't stop running until she was back at her garden gate.

From that day onwards, Goldilocks always listened to what her mummy told her. Although she heard that birdsong many times after, she never again wandered into the woods on her own.

Text 30

When Goldilocks Went to the House of the Bears

When Goldilocks went to the house of the bears,
Oh, what did her blue eyes see?
A bowl that was huge, and a bowl that was small
And a bowl that was tiny, and that was all,
She counted them one, two, three.

When Goldilocks went to the house of the bears,
Oh, what did her blue eyes see?
A chair that was huge, and a chair that was small
And a chair that was tiny, and that was all,
She counted them one, two, three.

When Goldilocks went to the house of the bears,
Oh, what did her blue eyes see?
A bed that was huge, and a bed that was small
And a bed that was tiny, and that was all,
She counted them one, two, three.

When Goldilocks went to the house of the bears,
Oh, what did her blue eyes see?
A bear that was huge, and a bear that was small
And a bear that was tiny, and that was all,
She counted them ROARRR, roarrr, roarrr!

Text 31

Goldilocks's Letter to the Three Bears

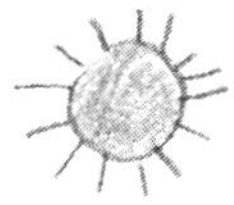

Dear Mr and Mrs Bear
and Baby Bear,

I am very sory indeed that I cam into your house and ate Baby Bears porij. Mummy says I am a bad girl. I hardly eat any porij when she cooks it she says. Daddy says he will mend the littel chair.

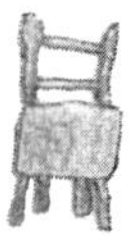

Love from
Goldilocks

P.S. Baby Bear can come to my party if he likes. Ther will be 3 kinds of jelly and a conjoora.

Text 32

Goldilocks's Envelope

Goldilocks and the Three Bears

Play Information

Characters:
Goldilocks
Daddy Bear
Mummy Bear
Baby Bear
Bird
Narrator

Key to characters:

Goldilocks

Daddy Bear

Mummy Bear

Baby Bear

Bird

Narrator

Props: table, table cloth, three different sized bowls, three different sized chairs, three different sized rugs, dress, bear masks, bird-call whistle.

Setting: The play is set in the middle of the woods in Fairytale Forest.

Scene 1: Outside Goldilocks's house.

Scene 2: At the Three Bears' house.

Scene 3: In the bedroom of the bears.

Text 34

Goldilocks and the Three Bears – The Play

Scene 1: Outside Goldilocks's house.

N : Once upon a time there lived three bears. Let me introduce them to you – Daddy Bear,

 : **ROAR!!!**

N : Mummy Bear,

 : ROAR

N : and little baby bear.

 : roar.

N : The three bears lived in a house deep in Fairytale Forest. At the edge of the forest there lived a little girl called Goldilocks.

 : Hello, I'm Goldilocks. Mummy says I mustn't wander off in the woods on my own, but can you hear that beautiful bird singing in the trees?

 : Tweet, tweet, tweety, tweet,
Follow me, follow me,
Singing high up in the tree,
Follow, follow, follow me!

N : At the same time, the three bears decided to go out for a walk to let their porridge cool down, because it was too hot to eat. As Goldilocks followed the bird into the woods, the three bears strolled into the trees for their early morning walk.

 : Tweet, tweet, tweety, tweet,
Follow me, follow me,
Singing high up in the tree,
Follow, follow, follow me!

Text 35

Goldilocks and the Three Bears – The Play (continued)

Scene 2: At the Three Bears' House.

: Where am I? I've never been this far into the woods before... Oh! What a sweet little cottage! I wonder who lives there? The door is open so I'll just have a little look inside. What a delicious smell – Mmmmm... porridge.

N : On the table were three bowls. A big bowl, a middle-sized bowl with roses around the rim and a little bowl with a pattern of pawprints. Goldilocks tasted the porridge in the big bowl.

: Too hot!

N : Goldilocks tasted the porridge in the middle-sized bowl.

: Too cold!

N : Then she tasted the porridge in the little bowl.

: Mmmmmmm, just right. That was delicious. I think I'll just have a rest, I'm sure no one will mind. Let me try this big wooden chair, I'll try to climb up onto it... Oh, too hard.

N : Next, Goldilocks tried the middle-sized chair, which was soft and red.

: Too soft!

N : And finally she tried the little chair, carved of wood. That chair was just right but with a horrible splintering sound, CRACK, the chair broke.

: I'm so tired, I think I'll have a little rest upstairs as none of these chairs will do.

N : Goldilocks crept up the creaking staircase.

Text 36

Goldilocks and the Three Bears – The Play (continued)

Scene 3: In the bedroom of the bears.

: Wow! What a big bed. But it is much too hard.

N : Next Goldilocks tried the middle-sized bed with the patchwork cover.

: Too soft! That little bed in the corner looks just right for me – I'll just have a little rest…

N : Goldilocks snuggled down and soon she was fast asleep.

Meanwhile, the bears had finished their walk in the woods and had come back home for breakfast. They looked at their bowls.

: **SOMEBODY'S BEEN EATING MY PORRIDGE!**

: SOMEBODY'S BEEN EATING MY PORRIDGE.

: **Somebody's been eating MY porridge – and they've eaten it all up!**

: **SOMEBODY'S BEEN SITTING IN MY CHAIR!**

: SOMEBODY'S BEEN SITTING IN MY CHAIR.

: **Somebody's been sitting in my chair and they've b-b-b-broken it! WAH!**

N : The three bears marched upstairs.

: **SOMEBODY'S BEEN SLEEPING IN MY BED!**

: SOMEBODY'S BEEN SLEEPING IN MY BED.

: **Somebody's been sleeping in my bed – and she's still there!**

N : At the sound of such growly voices, Goldilocks woke up. She saw three furry faces looking down at her! Goldilocks jumped out of bed and ran away as fast as her legs would carry her. From that day onwards, Goldilocks always listened to what her mummy told her.

SONG (ALL): "When Goldilocks went to the House of the Bears"

Text 37

Here Come the Aliens

A fleet of spaceships heads this way,
They're fifty zillion miles away
But getting closer every day –
The aliens are coming!

They're zooming in from outer space
To conquer us, the human race.
We'll soon be standing face to face –
The aliens are coming!

Colin McNaughton

Text 38

Here Come the Aliens (continued)

None speak English, French or Greek.
They sort of grunt and burp and squeak.
The chance of peace talks? I'd say BLEAK!
The aliens are coming!

Some have teeth and some are gummy,
Some are smart and some are dummy,
Some have... HELP! I want my mummy!
The aliens are coming!

Some are tall and some are squat,
Some are cool and some are hot,
Some are nice but most are not!
The aliens are coming!

Colin McNaughton

Text 39

Here Come the Aliens (continued)

At last the Earth comes into view.
The admiral knows what to do.
He orders, "BATTLE STATIONS, CREW!"
The aliens are coming!
BUT!
Approaching planet Earth, they see:
...
A piece of paper, floating free.
The aliens are slowing!

It's swiftly passed around the fleet.
A thousand hearts stop – miss a beat.
The order goes out: "FLEET RETREAT!!!"
The aliens are going!

Colin McNaughton

Text 40

Here Come the Aliens (continued)

For this is what the aliens saw:
A picture of your class – aged four!
It's scared them off – away they roar –
The aliens are going!

Yes all the aliens agree,
Of life in every galaxy,
The ugliest is you and me!
The aliens have gone, vamoosed –
The aliens have gone!

Colin McNaughton

Text 41

Character Profile – Alien

ALIEN ALERT

Police have discovered a huge crater in the woods close to this school. Hidden in the undergrowth was an empty spaceship...

Have you seen this alien?

Name:	Flobblegoop
Address:	Planet Zogg
Description:	Green and hairy, three eyes on stalks, long blue tongue, claws
Language spoken:	Zoggish. "Oggly bloop toggleytro Flobblegoop."
Likes:	Hiding in Year 1 classrooms, spider sandwiches, slug stew
Dislikes:	School dinners, spelling tests

If you see this alien in your school, please contact your head teacher immediately.

Text 42

From The Bed Book

Most Beds are Beds
For sleeping or resting,
But the *best* Beds are much
More interesting!

Not just a white little
Tucked-in-tight little
Nighty-night little
Turn-out-the-light little
Bed –

Instead
A Bed for Fishing,
A Bed for Cats,
A Bed for a Troupe of
Acrobats

The *right* sort of Bed
(If you see what I mean)
Is a Bed that might
Be a Submarine

Nosing through water
Clear and green,
Silver and glittery
As a sardine

Or a Jet-Propelled Bed
For visiting Mars
With mosquito nets
For shooting stars...

Sylvia Plath

Text 43

The Fiercest Dragon

Part One

Long, long ago and far, far away lived the dragons of the land of fairy tales. Dragons so huge that their red heads peered over the tops of mountains. Dragons so long that their scaly tails lashed the lakes below. Dragons so fierce that their fiery flames scorched the forest floors. Dragons so fearless that they would snatch princesses from castles in the kingdoms of the bravest kings.

The fiercest dragon of all lived in a cave in the snowy mountains. One winter's day, he uncoiled his forked tail, flexed his razor-sharp claws and stretched his long neck out of the cave to sniff the forest air for the faintest whiff of a princess. "Mmmmmm," he said to himself, "I could just eat a tasty princess with long hair. Delicious."

The fiercest dragon of all flew out of his lair and soared above the mountains looking for his dinner.

Far below, a princess sat weeping at the window of her turreted tower. The fiercest dragon of all pricked up his ears at the strange sound. As he flew closer to take a look, he saw the princess with her head in her hands.

"Oh woe is me, woe is me. I have been locked in this tower by a cruel witch and I can never, ever escape."

Text 44

The Fiercest Dragon

Part Two

Before he even had a chance to think twice, the fiercest dragon of all swooped down and snatched the princess from the stone window. He flew off, high into the winter sky.

As he neared his cave, the dragon thought to himself, "Well, just what shall I do now? Here I am with a tasty princess... but she is crying! I remember how sad I felt when I had to fly away from the family lair and how I shed big, green dragon tears."

The princess wriggled in the dragon's claws and looked him straight in the eye. The fiercest dragon of all sighed a huge sigh.

Gently, very gently, the fiercest dragon of all lowered the princess down to the entrance to his cave. The princess, who had got her Brownie Guide badge for camping, carefully swept the dragon's lair spick and span with a broom made of fir branches. She cooked a delicious roast bat dinner for them both and the dragon told the princess how lonely he had been. They became the very best of friends and, as in all the best fairy tales, they lived happily ever after.

Text 45

My Cat is...

A furry cat,
A whirry cat,
A soft and warm and purry cat.
A bouncy cat,
A pouncy cat,
A strutt around all flouncy cat.
A cheeky cat,
A sneaky cat,
A hide and seek and peeky cat.
A creepy cat,
A leapy cat,
An on my bed asleepy cat.

Text 46

Cat's Tongue

Cat's tongue,
Cat's tongue,
Pink as clover.

Cat's tongue,
Cat's tongue,
Wash all over.

Lick your paws,
Lick your face,
The back of your neck
And every place.

Lick your whiskers,
Smooth your fur,
Prick up your ears
And purr, purr, purr.

Cat's tongue,
Cat's tongue,
Pink as clover.

Cat's tongue,
Cat's tongue,
Clean all over.

Eve Merriam

Text 47

City Cat

City night,
Neon light,
Thin stray cat
Slips through the shadows
Eyes bright.
Scents each danger,
Wins each fight,
Then slips into the shadows,
Out of sight
Of eyes of men
In trains and cars
Racing homewards.
Licks her scars,
Then, eyes bright,
Tiptoes home
Into the night.

Text 48

Farm Cat

Tabby farm cat,
Ginger-wise,
Playing tigers in disguise,
Curls up on the cobbles.
Slowly stretches…
Coils…
And pounces
At a butterfly
That flutters by
High above the farmyard on a sunny afternoon.

Text 49

Miss Tibbles

Miss Tibbles is my kitten; white
as day she is and black as night.

She moves in little gusts and breezes
sharp and sudden as a sneeze is.

At hunting Tibbles has no match.
How I like to see her catch

moth or beetle, two a penny,
and feast until there isn't any!

Sometimes I like her calm, unwild,
gentle as a sleeping child,

and wonder as she lies, a fur ring,
curled upon my lap, unstirring, –
is it me or Tibbles purring?

Ian Serraillier

Text 50

Cats Sleep Anywhere

Cats sleep anywhere, any table, any chair.
Top of piano, window-ledge, in the middle,
on the edge.
Open draw, empty shoe, anybody's lap will do.
Fitted in a cardboard box, in the cupboard
with your frocks.
Anywhere! They don't care! Cats sleep anywhere.

Eleanor Farjeon

Teaching notes and ideas

TERM 1

Narrative 1

Stories with familiar settings

1–3 Lost in the Park

The story divides into a three-part structure which could be represented pictorially as a storyboard planner to plan children's own versions. The text would support the 'what next?' suggestions at the end of Developing Early Writing Unit 4.

1 Lost in the Park: Story Start

Talk with the class about the experience of getting lost and how this makes you feel. **T5, T9**

Explain to the class that you are going to write a new story, using this one as a model to help you. Model writing a story start in the first person, setting the scene and using 'I' for the pronoun. Support the class in writing their own first sentence(s). **S9**

2 Lost in the Park: Story Middle

Using the text as a stimulus, model writing the middle sentence(s) for your story, describing how you felt and using capital letters to show strength of feeling when lost. Support children's own composition. **S5**

3 Lost in the Park: Story End

Discuss with the class how the story ends happily and model a happy ending. Stick the three pages of text side by side on the board, and draw over them the story mountain or story sandwich model so that the class can see a physical representation of beginning, middle and end. Model and support children in writing a new story ending.

Poetry 1

Rhymes with predictable and repetitive patterns

4 Rhyme Dreams

This poem features a repeating verse pattern and predictable rhyme. It provides a model for linking the word level revision of cvc rhyming words to the text level objectives. **W1, W5, T6**. Sentence level objectives **S1, S2, S5** may also be taught through the text. Build a unit of work around the text, leading to an outcome of an independent or guided poem using the sentence frame 'A... in a... who is...', and inserting generated rhyme strings. **T10**

5 Sand

Another example of a poem using a highly structured pattern of a repeating sentence stem. This poem would lend itself to an outcome of a recited class poem, based on the shared text. **T4, T10**

Use the opportunity to link to phonics teaching and focus on the consonant cluster at the end of 'sand' for children working at this level. (Progression in Phonics Step 5.)

Narrative 2

Stories with familiar settings

6–8 Lion at School

This extract would support an outcome of a class wall story and oral retelling or role-play. The extract stops at a point that leads the class into continuing the story in their own familiar classroom setting, in drama or as a class story. Explain to the class that this story was written more than thirty years ago and it may well have been a story that their parents were read as a child. Discuss the traditional story language ('Once upon a time...', 'One morning...') and identify things that are the same today in classroom routines as they were when the story was written.

Explore at word level the reversal of 'lion' to 'noil', **W10**, and find funny reversed names in the class. Explore at sentence level the concept of a sentence being a complete idea and teach the difference between a line of text and a sentence, using Developing Early Writing pages 78–82 to support.

Scribe in discussion with the class over a series of lessons how the story might develop and end, set in your own classroom. Try using a repeating sentence start, for example, 'He didn't...' borrowed from the text. Build the developing story as a wall display story, enlarging the three pages of text and then adding new sentences each day as they are composed. Encourage the children to read the growing shared story to themselves and to others.

In independent and guided role-play, children are given guidance in acting out the developing story and presenting the final version in groups to each other.
T1, T2, T3, T7, S3, S5, S7

9–11 Sally and the magic rattle: the shore-people

This extract is another example of an 'older' text, one that lends itself to role-play.

Plan the unit of work to lead to a storytelling outcome, developing the children's concept of using the structure of a shared text as a basis for telling their own adventure stories.

The story is set in Sally's own house, in a cupboard. Make a physical representation of this in the classroom for role-play, using a curtain in a corner to build a story cupboard. To enhance the 'magical' vein of the storytelling, decorate the inside of the cupboard with coloured cellophane, shells, drapes or artefacts.

In shared work, read the text with the class, breaking the text into three sections.

9 Sally and the magic rattle: the shore-people

Discuss the story setting and the concept of 'safe' special places. Where do you go when you want to hide away quietly and read a book? **T5**.

Recite the magic rattle rhyme, exploring patterns of rhythm and rhyme. Use maracas to shake the rhythm in time to the rhyme. **T6**. The rhyme provides a useful opportunity to revise the double 'll' at the end of words (Progression in Phonics Step 3). **T1, T8**

In guided and independent work, support pupils to make up their own story starts based on key features of secret place setting, magic present and rhyme. Children may benefit from working with a response partner to share ideas with.

10 Sally and the magic rattle: the shore-people

The second section of text develops the story, taking Sally from her familiar setting to the setting of the shore-people. Model, as you read the text, how you are using the grammar of the sentences to help you read with expression and intonation. Try using a highlighter pen to mark the punctuation on the text, showing when reading how you are using it to tell you when to stop, to pause or to vary expression. **S3**

Relate how the story is developing to the 'story mountain' model and discuss the story dilemma.

Support the class in working in large guided groups (or as a class) to role-play the point where Sally meets the shore-people, using expression.

11 Sally and the magic rattle: the shore-people

In the third section, read and identify the resolution and ending with its twist in the tale. Challenge the class to think of any other stories that have the same trick of sending the character back to the real world with an object to make you think 'Was it true?' (John Burningham's *The Snowman*, Michael Foreman's *Jack's Fantastic Voyage*, Oxford Reading Tree 'Magic Key' adventures...)

Continue the unit through to a role-played outcome, with children working in groups to act out their magic rattle stories. **T7**

Poetry 2

Rhymes with predictable and repetitive patterns

12 Boa Constrictor

A very different type of poem to those in Poetry 1 (Texts 4 and 5), this time using repeating lines and rhyming couplets. Children in Year 1 respond enthusiastically to the anarchy of this poem and love the irreverent ending... Teach a unit leading to a spoken outcome, developing the expression and intonation needed to recite the poem effectively. **S3, T6**

TERM 2

Narrative 1

Traditional stories with familiar, predictable and patterned language

13–16 Jack and the Beanstalk

The traditional story of Jack and the Beanstalk provides a model for exploring both the traditional language of the text and the patterns of language. As a text structure, the tale has Jack repeatedly climbing the beanstalk, and the giant repeating the words 'Fee, fi, fo, fum'. Build with the class a visual storyline along a wall, working like a timeline, adding significant events along the line as you read the story. Highlight repeating features. **T14**

Work with the class to help them identify key features of story language (for example, 'Once upon a time…', 'happily ever after…'). **T5.**

Explore how the spoken text differs from the narrative in the story, **T4**, and use drama to develop conversation in the role of Jack's mother, or the giant's wife. Teacher and Teaching Assistant model how to extend this to hot seating, for example asking Jack's mother how she feels about her son having given the cow away. Develop through paired work. **T9**

17–19 Character Profiles

Try leading on from Jack and the Beanstalk (above) into a written unit, using text pages 18 and 19 to explore what a character profile is and then applying the text features to a chosen character from Jack and the Beanstalk. Model for the class how you will use what you have learnt from reading the story to help you build up a profile. Use a writing frame such as Text 17 to support children's own compositions. **T15**

Poetry

Traditional rhymes

20 The Three Little Pigs

This text organises the elements of a traditional tale into a rhyme format. Plan a short unit to link the work on traditional tales with this poetry unit on traditional rhymes, with an outcome of a class book of altered tales. Use to explore the patterns of rhyme and the elements of the traditional story.

Discuss with the class the reasons for and causes of incidents in the story, **T7**, and model for the class how the story can be adapted by altering these, for example 'What would happen if the three little pigs' Mummy had decided that she just couldn't bear her little piglets leaving home?', 'What could the wolf have done if he had a fear of heights? How else could he have tried to get in?' **T8**

Role-play new versions of the tale and make a class book of 'Twists in traditional tales'.

21 Twinkle Twinkle Little Star

The classic rhyme of 'Twinkle Twinkle' is an excellent example of how traditional rhymes lend themselves to adaptation. Learn and recite the original version, **T11**, then compare to Lewis Carroll's version from *Alice's Adventures in Wonderland*. Using the two versions of the rhyme together, highlight with a marker pen in one colour the words that are the same, and in a different colour the words that have changed.

Investigate initial consonant clusters such as 'star' with those children working on Progression in Phonics step 5. **W3**

Generate rhyme strings as a class using the pebble game (Progression in Phonics) for a range of words from appropriate phonics focus work such as 'fish' (cvc), 'feet' (long

vowel/ ee/), 'sink' (final consonant clusters), scribing the rhymes generated onto Post-it Notes™. Explore with the class how you can insert the Post-it Notes™ in place of the changed words, to make a new version with rhymes such as feet/eat, fish/wish, sink/think. For example, 'Twinkle, twinkle, little fish,
How I wonder what you wish!'

Identify with the class that the item to be changed in the fourth line can be very silly, but needs to look a little bit like the original 'Twinkle Twinkle' verse. The final two lines of the rhyme repeat the first two lines. As an outcome to the unit, children write their chosen new versions of 'Twinkle Twinkle' using the frame to support. **T12, T13**

22 What are Little Girls Made of?

A traditional rhyme that uses a repeating question in both verses, with the question answered in a rhyme. This rhyme would support a unit with an outcome of a new verse for the rhyme, based on the model. For example:

'What are little mice made of?
What are little mice made of?
Whiskers and nose
And tiny pink toes
That's what little mice are made of.' **T11, T13**

Narrative 2

Fairy stories from a range of cultures

23–25 Medio Pollito

A story from Spain that follows the traditional 'story mountain' model, though with a series of 'meetings' building up to the dilemma. It represents a 'moral' tale, with the selfish chicken being refused help himself at the end. It contains a repeating refrain, 'Oh no...for I am off to see the King of Spain. I will not help you' and the meetings would lend themselves well to exploration through drama.

Plan a story wall display to represent both the actual journey of the chicken, and the figurative journey of the story. Focus on one section of story each day, exploring the text and language features and composing a class version to add to the ongoing story display as the unit builds. Children could make their own story journeys in guided and independent time on a long strip of paper, adding the new developments in words and/or pictures each day. **T4, T9, T12, T15**

26–29 Goldilocks and the Three Bears

A traditional fairy tale, which many children will have heard told before. The structure of repeating events and spoken refrain make this a very accessible story for early writers. Encourage the class to act out the story, using different voices for the three bears. Explore how the font gives us a clue as to how to read the words, the bigger and bolder the lettering, the louder the voice. This will support the concept of playscript in the next unit. The story is presented in three sections – read and discuss key text and language features of each in turn. Model for the class how you will write your own sentence(s) for each section after analysing it and support the children in writing their own to build to a story outcome. **S4, S5, T5, T10, T12, T14, T16**

30–32 Goldilocks and the Three Bears – what happened next?

These texts support the Goldilocks unit as a 'What happened next?' discussion and unit extension. Consider making a 'Fairytale Forest' role-play area and model for the class how in play you can take the action on to imagine what might happen next. **T9**

Provide opportunities to explore 'what happened next?' in writing a letter to the bears from Goldilocks, using the extract from *The Jolly Postman* to stimulate play. **T16**

30 When Goldilocks Went to the House of the Bears

This text provides the lyrics to a well-known classroom song, with which to support the unit.

31 Goldilocks's Letter to the Three Bears

32 Goldilocks's Envelope

Plays

33 Goldilocks and the Three Bears – Play Information

The playscript of *Goldilocks and the Three Bears* relates very closely to the narrative version (Texts 26–29). Because the class will now be very familiar with the content of the story, and many of the text and language features, the focus in this unit is on understanding what a play is. Use the information page to discuss playscript conventions, and look at other examples to identify common features. **T8, T9**

34–36 Goldilocks and the Three Bears – The Play

Model in shared and guided reading how to read the playscript using all the clues from the information page and work towards a drama outcome using the script to support as the play develops. Try adopting a 'read scene 1, discuss scene 1, act scene 1' model on the first day, repeated on subsequent days for the other two scenes.

Children could work in groups of six to produce their own plays as spoken outcomes. Take the opportunities presented in this unit to develop practice in both speaking and listening, reinforcing what good speakers and listeners have to do. **T8, T9, S1, S4**

TERM 3

Narrative 1

Stories about fantasy worlds

37–40 Here Come the Aliens

This text engages young children through its 'fantasy' theme and comic rhyme. Plan an outcome of a class performance of the story, with accompaniment. Read the text with the class as a shared reading text, highlighting text and language features. Work with the class on visualising what these strange aliens might look like, using clues drawn from the text. Consider using ICT to support and involve the class in drawing what they imagine one of the aliens might look like on a drawing program such as *Paintbox* or *Colour Magic*. Use a copy of the complete illustrated text if available to compare what the children thought the aliens might look like to the illustrator's ideas.

Discuss with the class how authors use different settings to draw the reader into a story – we have never been into space so the setting is strange to us, or unfamiliar. Fifty zillion miles must be a long way! We will have to imagine what it is like, unlike the work on stories with familiar settings, when we were familiar with them. Find different examples of stories with fantasy settings and collect as a display.

The setting for this story is in a fleet of spaceships fifty zillion miles away – did the author choose a good setting for 'Here Come the Aliens'? Why? What other books have we read or films have we seen that use the same setting? Use musical instruments to accompany oral retelling of the story, and consider recording the performance to use again as a storytape. **T8, T10**

41 Character Profile – Alien

Extend this unit into a written outcome by reinforcing work on character profiles in Term 2. **T12, T13**

Poetry 1

Poems with patterned and predictable structures

42 *From* The Bed Book

Text 42 develops on from the very explicit predictable and repetitive patterns of the previous terms. In 'The Bed Book' extract, both repeating and rhyming patterns are used by the poet at various points in the poem. Explore the patterns with the class in shared reading, using different coloured highlighter pens to identify where the poet uses a) rhyme and b) repeating words or phrases. Discuss the poet's precise use of language, getting the children to close their eyes and picture the submarine 'Nosing through the water, Clear and green, Silver and glittery as a sardine.' Poems can paint pictures in the readers' minds with their words. Compare this verse to a 'boring' version – 'Going through the water like a fish'.

Play 'The Noun Game' with the class, giving them a simple noun such as a fish or a cat, and asking 'Where? What colour? What type? What was it doing? How was it moving?' type questions in order to find out more detail. Model on the board how you can do this in writing too, starting off with a simple noun and adding detail to create a much more vivid picture. Try playing this game orally with a different noun each day.

Plan an outcome of a class anthology of poems, where every child has contributed their favourite poem, discussing key features and why they like it. Use 'The Bed Book' text as the first poem in the collection, as a class favourite. Laminate the pages of the anthology when complete, to make a lasting classroom poetry book entitled:

> Some poems are poems
> For sleeping or resting
> But the best poems are much
> More interesting! **T10, T11, W8**

Narrative 2

Stories about fantasy worlds

43–44 The Fiercest Dragon

A short story with a 'moral' theme following a classic story structure. The story is written in four parts; beginning, build-up, dilemma, resolution and ending. Plan to read, analyse and write own versions of each section in turn, building to a written outcome. Refer back to the previous narrative unit on fantasy and compare settings. **T8**

This story is set somewhere else that we will have to imagine, in a cave in the snowy mountains, far away in the land of fairy tales. In the first part of the story, identify the traditional story language and setting and explore the author's use of the repeated phrase 'dragons so (adjective)' to build up suspense. What other adjectives could be used for dragons? In the story build-up, explore how the author has used precise language to transport the reader to the dragon's cave. Explore the differences between 'One day he got up and smelt the air' and 'One winter's day, he uncoiled his forked tail, flexed his razor-sharp claws and stretched his long neck out of the cave to sniff the forest air for the faintest whiff of a princess.' **T16**

Discuss with the class how the dragon and the princess would speak in very different voices and develop this in paired work. **S3**

In the story dilemma, the roles are reversed and we realise that the fiercest dragon of all isn't really very fierce after all. Explore through circle time the concept of feeling sad and make a class list of times we felt sad. Model using one of these in the demonstration writing of the dilemma.

Through the story resolution, relate this story ending to other 'happily ever after' endings. **T12, T13, T14**

Poetry 2

A variety of poems on similar themes

The following six texts are all linked by a theme of cats. **T9**

The poems are a deliberate mixture of styles to encompass a range of older poems by established poets and new modern poems. Compare and contrast several of the poems as a unit of work, giving preferences and explaining choices. **T10**

Compile (with any other examples from the class library collection and children's own compositions) a class anthology of cat poems. **T11**

45 My Cat is...

Discuss with the class how each line describes the pet cat. The lines are not complete sentences (they contain no verb) but all follow the pattern 'A (adjective) cat'. Using different coloured highlighter pens, highlight all 'A's in one colour, all the nouns (cat) in another colour, all the adjectives in a third colour and all the connectives (and) in a further colour. Explore with the class what other words could be used to fit in the adjective gaps, making a list of words that might fit and discussing why. **S4**

Explore the order of the phrases on whiteboards, applying the phonics being taught to particular groups through playing 'Sentence spell' (Developing Early Writing page 169) supporting the class in writing the sentences 'A........... cat' and inserting words to reinforce phonics, for example, 'bad' (step 4), 'black' (step 5), 'cool' (step 6).

Demonstrate for the class how you will apply these in writing a new poem based on the repeating pattern. Support children in writing their own new 'My cat is...' poems. **T9, T10, T15**

46 Cat's Tongue

This poem by Eve Merriam is a good poem to learn and recite as it has strong patterns of rhythm and rhyme. Investigate the two line repeat of 'Cat's tongue, Cat's tongue' followed by a rhyming line by composing a shared, guided or independent poem based on this pattern, for example,

Cat's tongue,	Cat's tongue,
Cat's tongue,	Cat's tongue,
Lick your paws	Lick your fur.
Cat's tongue,	Cat's tongue,
Cat's tongue,	Cat's tongue,
Stretch your claws	Purr, purr, purr.

T9, T10, T11, S3

47 City Cat

'City Cat' is an example of a poem that has all the 'unnecessary' words taken out, leaving only the powerful words that tell us of the life of a stray city cat. Explore with the class how in narrative the start of the poem might be 'It is night time in the city and a neon light is shining down on a thin stray cat with bright eyes who is slipping through the shadows.' In poetry, less is often more and because we are trying to paint a picture in the reader's mind, we can use only the words that are good for painting with! Another opportunity to link phonics into reading and writing for those children working at Step 7, exemplifying the long vowel phoneme /ie/ as /igh/. The 'igh' sound repeats as a rhyme for 'night' at intervals throughout the poem. **T10, T11**

48 Farm Cat

This poem provides a contrast to the city cat in Text 47. It provides some unusual vocabulary to investigate linked to movement ('curls', 'stretches', 'coils', 'pounces', 'flutters'). **T10, W8**

49 Miss Tibbles

Compare the poem to other examples of poems about cats. What does Miss Tibbles have in common with the previous cats? Identify links of cat movements, hunting prey, curled up sleeping, purring. Poets who write about cats often refer to these characteristics. Reinforce sentence level objective for Year 1 Term 3 and teach the use of capitalisation for personal titles (Miss Tibbles). **T10, S5**

50 Cats Sleep Anywhere

This poem by Eleanor Farjeon is written as a list poem, listing the places where cats like to sleep. The poet uses pairs of short rhyming lines to give a pattern to the poem. **T9, T10, T11**

Compare and contrast with other cat poems and end the unit with a 'Booker Cat Poem Prize' competition with all the poems in the anthology displayed and numbered. Model for the class how to give reasons for your own personal favourite, and encourage other adults visiting the classroom to do the same. Model how giving reasons for liking something needs to be more specific than 'because I do' or 'because it is good'. Refer back to the text and language features as reasons for your choice, for example 'This poem is my favourite because I like the way the poet describes the way the cat moves. It reminds me of my cat when she is chasing a leaf.' Make a class ballot box and show the children how you write the number of your favourite poem on a slip of paper to vote. Give all children their opportunity to vote for their favourite poem, expressing the reasons for their choice as they vote.